balconies

architectural details

Imprint
The Deutsche Bibliothek is registering
this publication in the Deutsche National-
bibliographie; detailed bibliographical
information can be found on the internet
at http://dnb.ddb.de

ISBN 978-3-938780-48-0 (Hardcover)
ISBN 978-3-938780-17-6 (Softcover)

© 2008 by Verlagshaus Braun
www.verlagshaus-braun.de

1st edition 2008

Editor:
Markus Sebastian Braun
Editorial staff:
Julia Goltz, Annika Schulz
Translation:
Alice Bayandin
Graphic concept and layout:
Michaela Prinz

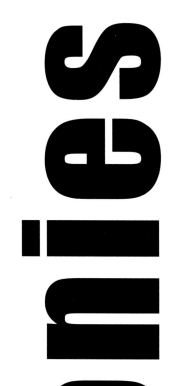

balconies

architectural details

BRAUN

contents

lisbon, parque das nações (parque expo 98)

balconies – urban views

How many different associations the balcony evokes in us! Perhaps to begin, we should dryly state just what a balcony is, and what it is not. The word balcony comes from Middle High German *balko*, meaning beam. It is a platform made out of stone, today often replaced by reinforced concrete, which protrudes freely from a building wall at the level of one of its stories. Because walking outside at head-spinning elevations is associated with a number of dangers, the platform is enclosed with a low wall or a balustrade composed of small pillars or bars. Early balustrades, like balconies themselves, were made of stone; for today's balustrades, metal is often the material of choice. The balcony is characterized by its lack of roofing, which differentiates it from a loggia that is closed in on three sides and opens up only at the front, and from a bay, which is closed all around, being merely an externally overhanging interior space.

Balconies fulfilled and to this day fulfill an array of purposes. Firstly, they offer an opportunity to contemplate the surroundings and take in fresh air without having to leave the house. In 1771, in his *General Theory of the Fine Arts*, Johann Georg Sulzer proclaimed: "Balconies mainly allow us to walk out into the fresh air to be able to comfortably take a look around. To serve this purpose safely and to prevent falling down, they are supplied with a banister. They are generally placed at the level of the second floor at the center of the exterior façade, thus supplying this part of the building with more grandeur."

The so-called "economy balconies" served as additional space for household activities like hanging the wash to dry, chilling of dishes or storing buckets of water to control house fires, much to the chagrin of the neighbors at this not-so-uplifting view. As an urban planning element, the green balcony served more and more often the role of a garden replacement for city residents. We will later touch upon "decorative balconies", too.

The tranquility associated with its later use lets us forget that the balcony, originating in the 13th and 14th centuries in European residential architecture, has its roots in defence parapets of medieval castles. At the top of a city wall these parapets had to be wide enough to let soldiers walk in both directions without stepping on each other. For this reason a widening at the top of the wall in the direction of the inner yard was constructed using wooden planks or projecting stone plates. In the late Middle Ages the expanded battlements protruded on both sides of the wall. Floor openings on the side of the hang facing the external wall called machicolations were used to pour scalding water, oil, tar and arrows from the extremely advantageous angle on the besieging party. Additional external building protrusions were the feared garderobes, through which excrement was conveniently released into the moat below.

The elaborately and lovingly designed decorative balconies of the Renaissance were tailored to the lifestyle and elegance of the age, closer approaching the balcony's modern use. For many years the altan (from It.: turret) or solarium, a balcony platform which rested on pillars or supports that reached the ground, outpaced the balcony, whose free-floating nature left some feeling less than secure. The difference between the solarium and the balcony was also blurred in language, since both served the same purpose. From the 242-volume *Economical Encyclopedia* (1773-1858) from Johann Georg Krünitz on the subject of the balcony: "A place lying above the house and under the skies, meant as a location for pleasure and amusement from which a green perspective onto the fields presents itself in the summertime, and where flowers and other plants can be placed. For many persons come onto this place, it must be enclosed with a banister."

With this we reach the definition of the balcony's main purpose as a garden replacement. Balcony architecture is found primarily in large cities, often in rental slums built using the generalizing formula for high-density apartment buildings. In 1900 the quickly-expanding Berlin was already known as Europe's balcony capital. The victory march of the geranium and other common potted plants went hand in hand with modernity's preferred way of dealing with nature in the city. Green balconies entailed making sacks of potting soil, buying of plants, raking, weeding, watering and pest control a part of urban life in the balcony garden. This location is hailed to this day by gardening suppliers as the "paradise with a banister", "five meters of happiness" and the "oasis in the high-rise". Or, depending on the audience, the balcony garden culture is declared to be the torch of the ecological movement's resistance to the monotony of the concrete jungle.

Many balcony fans are bothered by unsteady weather and seasonal cold limiting the use of their home garden. Complete glazing of the balcony aids the situation. Glass is simply inserted into the metal frame of the balcony and made continuous with the balcony above. In good weather, all glass elements can be opened or folded away, while in the closed state a cross between a balcony and a bay suited for year-round use results. One can even find balconies with a floor made of unbreakable glass, which allows a view below. This complete feeling of hovering above the street is not for everyone, and can awaken queasiness in some.

Failures of a poorly-maintained balcony resulting in a fall to one's death from a ramshackle platform are a rare occurrence, but notices thereof appear here and there in the papers. The situation feeds one of man's primary fears, the feeling of complete helplessness. The film industry experimented with this genre, for example in the 1961 filming of an Edgar Wallace classic *The Weird Countess*. In the house of the countess a girl named Lois walks through a door which should have stayed closed at all times. She lands on a run-down balcony that immediately falls apart under her weight. The helpless screaming girl hanging on for her life to the house's wall is saved not a moment too soon.

In general, however, the balcony enjoys a positive image in the cultural and historical sense, especially where proclamations of love are concerned. This includes images of the lover rapidly descending from a rope thrown from a balcony after the unexpected return of the husband. Another cliché is the troubadour in love who serenades the object of his affections with poems, songs and the rapid beats of his heart, awaiting that she comes out onto the balcony and listens to him. The romantic hero does not use the door when entering a house; instead, rose between his teeth, he climbs up the wall along conveniently placed ivy climbers, drain pipes and trees, all leading to the balcony where the loved one shall be shortly conquered.

The most famous balcony in the history of romance, or at least in the history of literature, is found in Verona, more exactly on no. 27 Via Capello. Supposedly this is where the house of Juliet's parents from William Shakespeare's *Romeo and Juliet* once stood, and the enthusiasm of the love tourists is not in the least extinguished by the fact that its balcony was added only later. In the second scene of the drama's second act Juliet steps out on her balcony and in a soliloquy confesses her love for Romeo. At this, the young man who has been hiding in the garden during the speech emerges, declaring his love for her. This is the start of the tragic and deadly love between the offspring of the houses of Montague and Capulet, which leads to the families' reconciliation only over the lovers' corpses.

Balconies also play a role in international politics, although today the sight of a royal family benevolently waving to their subjects from a balcony seems rather casual.
When white smoke appears from the chimney in the Vatican after a successful election of a new pope, the eyes of not just Catholics, as was earlier the case, but of the whole world turn to look at the St. Peter's balcony, or loggia. Here, the oldest cardinal deacon appears and pronounces the famous words: "Annuncio vobis gaudium magnum: Habemus Papam! – I announce to you a great joy: We have a Pope!" With this, he says the name of

the chosen cardinal, as well as his papal name. The new Pontifex Maximus steps out onto the balcony and blesses the Urbi et Orbi – the city of Rome and its surroundings – for the first time.

And what conclusion can we draw from the balcony's many functions? In 1934 the vocalist ensemble Comedian Harmonists had a hit song whose lyrics spoke of the tranquility of the green balcony and the hardiness of its owner, while contemplating on the original legacy of the parapet in facilitating the falling (or throwing) down of objects from the right angle. "My small green cactus is standing out on the balcony, heyea, heyo, hayee! Why should I want red roses, why should I want red poppies…" and there it stands, until one day the doorbell rings and "Mister Kraus from the next house" asks "Don't you have a small green cactus standing on the balcony, heyea, heyo, hayee! It just fell down below, what do you think of this? Heyea, heyo, hayee!" The awkwardness stems from the fact that the cactus fell right on Mister Kraus' face, resulting in the victim's urgent advice: "Do me a favor, and keep your cactus somewhere else, heyea, heyo, hayee!" But to this day there is nowhere the balcony owner would rather have his plants but "out on the balcony".

Markus Hattstein

amsterdam

amsterdam, oosterdokskade

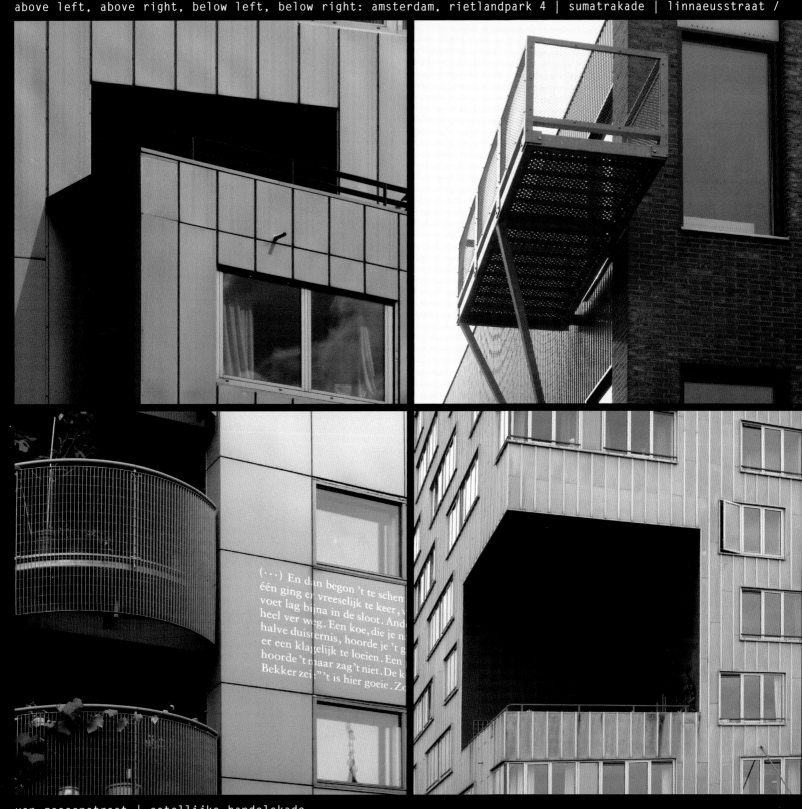

(···) En dan begon 't te schem
één ging er vreeselijk te keer,
voet lag bijna in de sloot. And
heel ver weg. Een koe, die je n
halve duisternis, hoorde je 't g
er een klagelijk te loeien. Een
hoorde 't maar zag 't niet. De k
Bekker zei:"'t is hier goeie. Zo

amsterdam, leidsekade 57-67

amsterdam, rietlandpark 4

kadijk 117-124 | jan luijkenstraat 56

athens

athens, tzortz 4

above left, above right, below left, below right: athens, eleftheriou venizelou 16 | eleftheriou venizelou 18 | ippokratous 1 | korai 5

athens, georgiou a'

barcelona, passeig de gracia 92

barcelona, rambla de sant josep 35

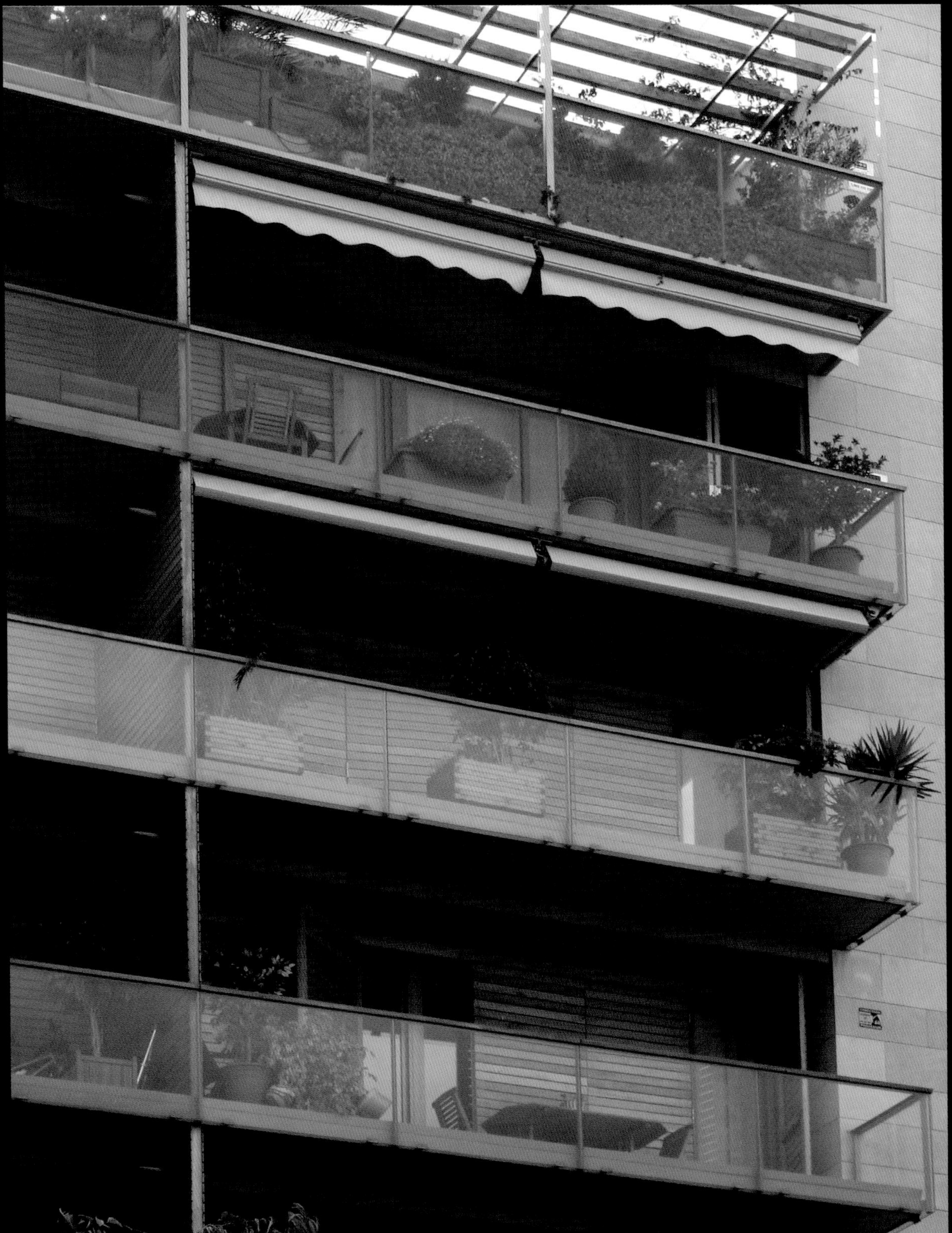

barcelona, rambla del poblenou 125-127

sant josep 55 | avenida marquès de comillas 13 (poble español de montjuïc) | avenida marquès de comillas 13
(poble español de montjuïc)

berlin

berlin, sony center

linkstraße 8-10

above left, above right, below left, below right: berlin, zimmerstraße 19 | herbert-von-karajan-straße 1 | herbert-von-karajan-straße 1 | herbert-von-karajan-straße 1

berlin, am park 4

berlin, marlene-dietrich-platz

left, above right, below right: berlin, sony center | in den ministergärten | sony center

berlin, wilhelmstraße 140

berlin, stresemannstraße 60

berlin, marlene-dietrich-platz

berlin, rykestraße 13

above left, above right, below left, below right: berlin, leipziger straße 43,44 | manteuffelstraße 6 |

choriner straße 2 | knaackstraße 22

brussels

brussels, rue de parnasse 31

brussels, rue de francs

budapest, honvéd utca 3

szabadság tér 15

above left, above right, below left, below right: budapest, eötvös utca 31 | eötvös utca 31 | eötvös utca 31 | király utca 74 | ix. üllöi út 33-37 (iparművészeti múzeum)

50

budapest, ix. üllöi út 33-37 (iparmüvészeti múzeum)

budapest, puskás ferenc stadion

above left, above right, below left, below right: budapest, csaba utca 5 | ditró utca 6 | várfok utca 15b |

napraforgó utca 2

copenhagen

copenhagen, kalvebod brygge 27

left, above right, below right: copenhagen, snorresgade 7a | myggenæsgade 30 | myggenæsgade 30

copenhagen, jens otto krags gade 14

copenhagen, jens otto krags gade 5

left, above right, below right: copenhagen, kalvebod brygge 35 | arsenaloen 66 | o2

copenhagen, stoltenbergsgade 1

copenhagen, myggenæsgade 25

above left, below left, right: copenhagen, hans hedtofts gade 6 | teglholmsgade | myggenæsgade 34

copenhagen, sturlasgade 9

drechselsgade 20-24 | artillerivej 44

cracow, ulica wielopole 6

above left, above right, below left, below right: cracow, plac na groblach 11 | ulica kopernika 25 | ulica św. gertrudy 3 | ulica szpitalna 40

cracow, ulica zwierzyniecka 30

helsinki

helsinki, abrahaminkatu

above left, below left, right: helsinki, thakontie | runeberginkatu | itainenpapinkatu

helsinki, mechelininkatu

istanbul, sultan ahmed camii / ahmediye camii

above left, above right, below left, below right: istanbul, divanyolu caddesi | istiklal caddesi | buyuk hendek caddesi | iskele caddesi

istanbul, istiklal caddesi

istanbul, prof k.i. gurkan caddesi

h'davendigar caddesi | küçük ayasofya caddesi / tavukhane sokak

lisbon

lisbon, parque das nações (parque expo 98)

parque das nações (parque expo 98)

above left, above right, below left, below right: lisbon, parque das nações (parque expo 98) | pereira de malo 19 | avenida sidonio pais | avenida columbano bordalo pinheiro 55

lisbon, parque das nações (parque expo 98)

lisbon, avenida da republica 87

avenida da republica 38a | rua braamcamp 40

above left, above mid, below mid, right: lisbon, rua do alecrim 26 | parque das nações (parque expo 98) | parque das nações (parque expo 98) | parque das nações (parque expo 98) | parque das nações (parque expo 98) | parque das nações (parque expo 98) |

ljubljana, riharjeva ulica 19

above left, below left, right: ljubljana, aškerčeva ulica 5 | miklošičeva cesta 3 (grand hotel union business) |

tabor 9 (hotel park)

above left, above right, below left, below right: ljubljana, miklošičeva cesta 18 | hribarjevo nabrežje | hribarjevo nabrežje | tavčarjeva ulica 8a

ljubljana, kongresni trg 10 (slovenska filharmonija)

ljubljana, prešernov trg 5/6

ulica 21 | stari trg 34

london

london, 29 st. martin's lane

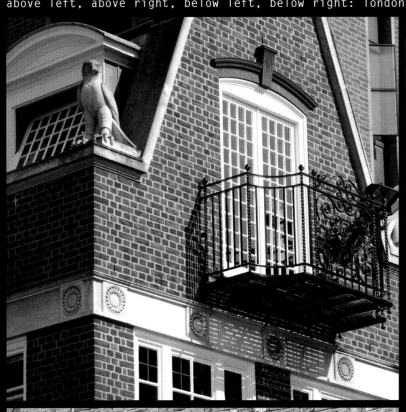

66 pont street

above left, above right, below left, below right: london. threadneedle street (bank of england) | 2 pembridge gardens | 55 kensington park road | 60 hyde park gate (baglioni hotel)

london, 28 shad thames (design museum)

58 chepstow villas

left, right: london, silk street (the barbican centre) | bankside

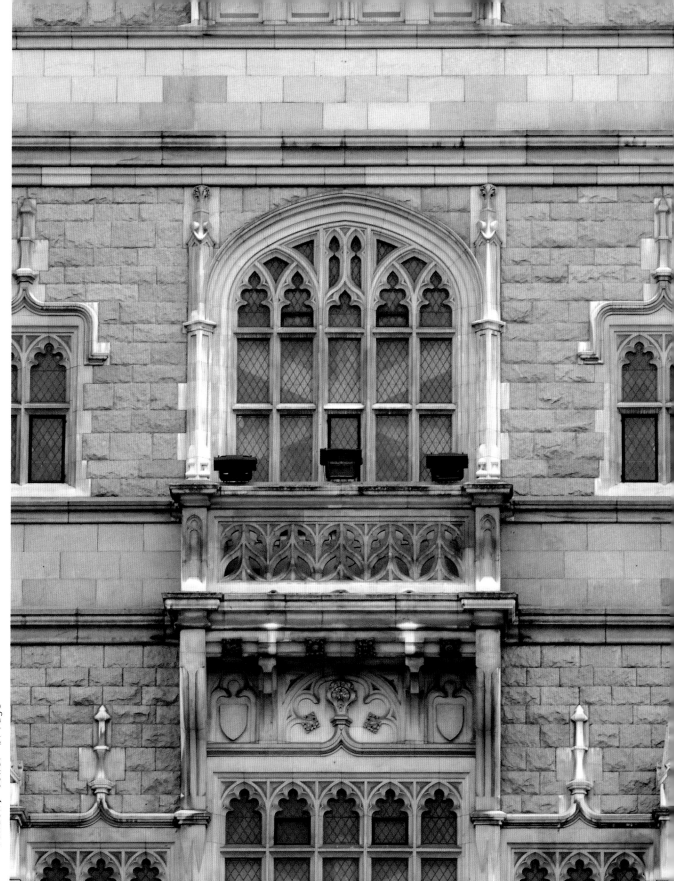

london, tower bridge

paris, 8-20 rue raymond aron

Les Tissus de Qualité

MARCHÉ SAINT-PIERRE

montmartre | 2 rue des écoles

above left, above right, below left, below right: paris, 19 boulevard jourdan (cité internationale universitaire de paris) | 1 rue azaïs | 1 rue azaïs | 13 rue des écoles

paris, 21 boulevard diderot

paris, 40 boulevard haussmann (galeries lafayette)

prague

prague, stroupežnického 21

above left, above right, below left, below right: prague, arcibiskupský palác | masarykovo nábřeží 2 | haštalská 4 | královská zahrada

prague, celetná 29

prague, václavské náměstí 25

riga, kungu ielā 9

above left, above right, below left, below right: riga, antonijas ielā | teātra ielā 2 | citadeles ielā | jurmala

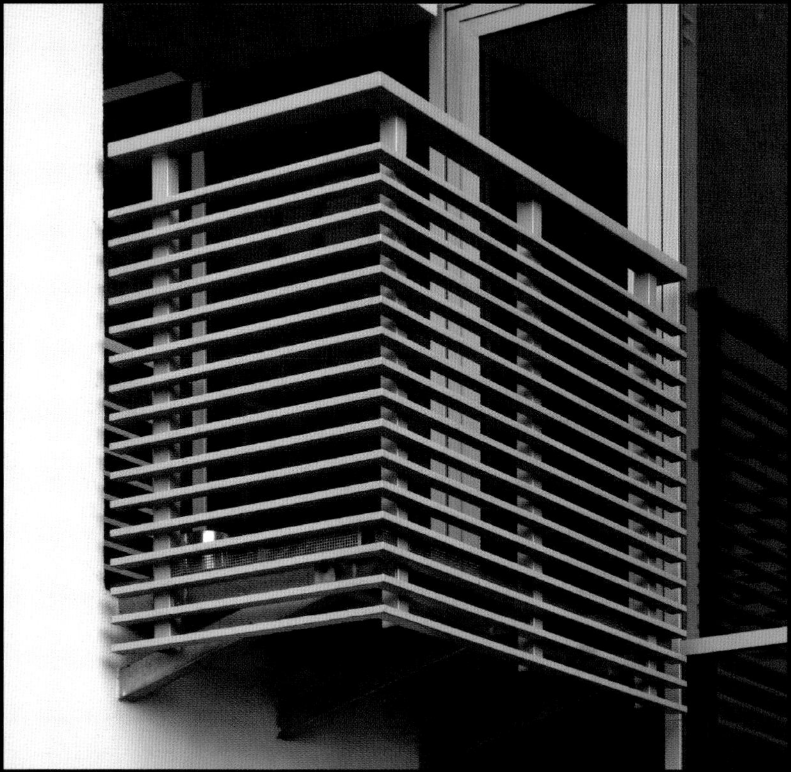

above left, above right, below left, below right: riga, strelnieku ielā 4a | alberta ielā 12a | pils laukums 4 | elisabetes ielā 10b

riga, elisabetes ielā 10b

brieža ielā

rome

rome, piazzale degli archivi

viale dell' arte 44

above left, above right, below left, below right: rome, largo gaetana agnesi | via buonarroti 41 | via san giovanni in laterano 28 | viale della civiltà romana

rome, via francesco giambullari 8

poliziano 61 | viale america 359 | viale europa

stockholm

stockholm, bondegatan 74

above left, above right, below left, below right: stockholm, kocksgatan 41 | hötorget 8 (konserthuset) | kungsbron 21 | liljeholmen

stockholm, klippgatan 16

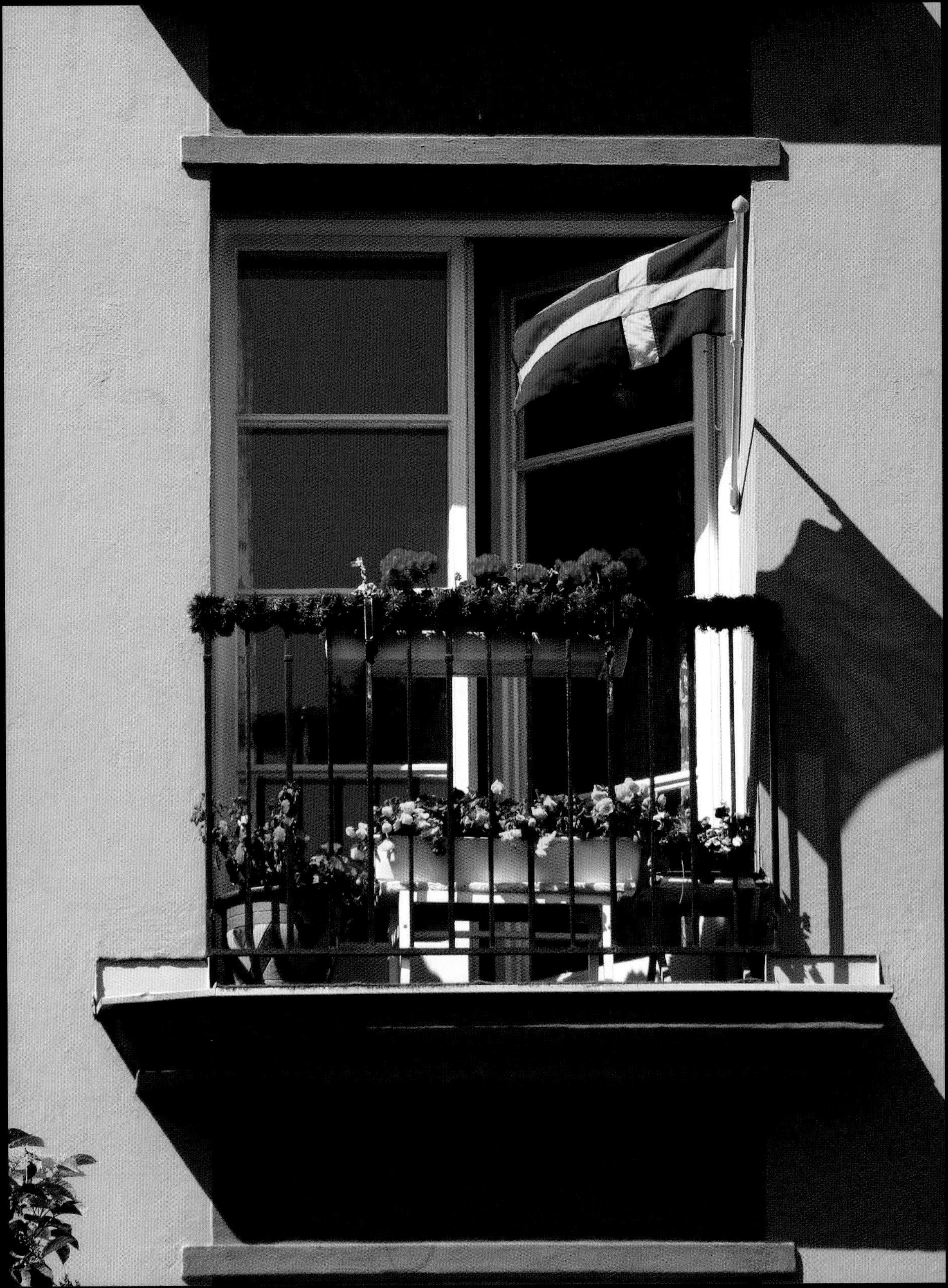

stockholm, asögatan 173

tulegatan 6 | tegnergatan 41

above left, above right, below left, below right: stockholm, engelbrektsgatan 37 | odengatan | södra
blasieholmshamnen | drottninggatan 33 (stadshuset)

stockholm, rådmansgatan 35

st. petersburg, ul. tschernyschevskogo 3

above left, above right, below left, below right: st. petersburg, 5. krasnoarmeijskaja ul. 12 |

bolschaja konjuschennaja ul. 15 | karavannaja ul. 2 | nevskij prospekt 66

above left, above right, below left, below right: st. petersburg, bolschaja konjuschennaja ul. 5 | nevskij prospekt (gastini dvor) | karavannaja ul. 8 | klinski prospekt 15

st. petersburg, ul. warschavskaja 23

st. petersburg, malaja konjuschennaja ul. 5

kirotshnaja ul. 24 | nevskij prospekt 40

vienna

vienna, carl appelstraße 7

hertha-firnberg-straße 7 | hertha-firnberg-straße 10

vilnius

above left, above right, below left, below right: vilnius, aušros vartų 13 | aušros vartų 5 (nacionalinė filharmonija) | bokšto gatvė 19/12 | krivių gatvė 5

vilnius, l. stuokos-gucevičiaus gatvė 3

jono basanavičiaus gatvė 16 | didžioji gatvė 35/2

zurich

zurich, tannenstrasse 8

rämistrasse 71 (universität zürich) | schiffbauerstrasse 11

above left, below left, right: zurich. limmatquai 27 | limmatquai 29 | zollikerstrasse 130

zurich, limmatquai 19

photographers index

claudia bull   st. petersburg
www.bulldesign.de

**"to photograph something you need time.
if you don't have time, you can make snapshots."**

dominik butzmann   helsinki
www.dbutzmann.de

**"what a dream – to wander the streets without a map, without
a schedule and collect impressions, colors, faces, light and
shadow!"**

marius flucht   amsterdam, berlin
www.herrflucht.de

"look!"

katja hoffmann   ljubljana, london, vilnius
www.katjahoffmann.de

**"without my camera I would have given up wanting to
understand the world."**

thomas kierok   barcelona, vienna, zurich
www.kierok.de

"seeing is the way to awareness."

johannes kramer   athens, budapest, prague
johannes.kramer@berlin.de

"photography for me is a confrontation with reality –
an interplay between objectivity and fantasy."

marion lammersen   paris
www.marionlammersen.com

"symbiosis of art and nature creates authentic and interesting
architecture."

bernhardt link   istanbul, rome
www.link-foto.de

"photographs reveal their own reality, or that, what the
photographer considers as such."

kai senf   berlin, brussels, copenhagen
www.kaisenf.com

"the organization and engineering of any architecture I perceive
in my viewfinder suggests a feeling of order that contrasts
the storm that is going on in my head. architecture photography
has a very meditative and calming effect on me."

claudia weidemann   lisbon, riga, stockholm
c.weidemann@berlin.de

"photography changes my perception of reality."

katja zimmermann   cracow
office@beta-75.com

"architecture itself carries stories out of the
centuries past behind the façades – photographs of
architecture tell us completely new stories."